The Unshackled Soul: A Shy Gal's Guide to Self-Confidence

By

Lindsay Brant-Brumwell

Table of Contents

DEDICATION – Lindsay Brant-Brumwell

I'd like to dedicate this book to everyone who has ever believed in me, and my gift of writing. I am so blessed to have many incredible people in my life. To list each one of you individually would be challenging, and I most certainly would not want to leave anyone out. I think you know who you are.

To my husband, Dan, and son Colson, thank you for your patience and support during the writing process. Thank you for your love, your kindness, and your inspiration.

To my sisters, Brittany and Emily, and parents Cathy and Marlin, thank you for your constant encouragement and reminders to use my gift. To my Dad, in particular, who always said, "I want you to write a book so that I can read it."

This is also dedicated to my grandparents, Jacqueline and Glenn. Thank you for encouraging me. I share my love for the written word with you, Gram, and I believe my writing talents were passed down to me from you.

To my grandparents on my mother's side, Muriel and Clarence, who would have been so proud to see this book published, and to know that I am following my heart and using the gifts that God has given me.

Special thanks to those of you that offered advice and assistance during the revision process. Thanks to Anne Marie, my Jedi Master, for offering her editorial eye and endless encouragement during this, and other projects I've done. I hope you continue to call me "Young Padawan" even when I'm older!

Special thanks to those friends of mine who I've quoted throughout the book. Your comments have inspired me, whether you meant them to or not.

To all of my teachers, who instilled in me a sense of confidence, and supported me during times when my self-belief was fleeting. There are a handful of you that impacted my life far beyond your calling as educators and for that I am grateful. Special thanks to all of my elementary school teachers, high school English teachers, and my University professors. Thank you to Kathleen, in particular, for inspiring and uplifting a young girl, and for being the reason for this book's existence.

Thank you to my writer friends and colleagues for their unwavering support, encouragement, advice, and belief in me.

I lift this book up to you, God, as a thank you for giving me the gift of writing, and for allowing me to follow my dreams and the plans you have made for me.

Introduction

The goal of this book is to help other shy individuals learn how to overcome their shyness. As I was growing up I was painfully shy. I would avoid social situations, and often my face would blush during even the slightest interaction with others. This book will offer my personal advice and outline steps you can take to break free of the shackles of shyness and live a life that is true to yourself. Shyness presents itself in individuals around the world, and the root cause of shyness is fear. Fear is the opposition to beauty in life. Fear can paralyze us and prevent us from changing and growing. It is necessary first to conquer our fears, and in doing so, we can conquer our shyness.

You may be wondering what qualifies me to write this book. Why should a gal like me be telling you about how to overcome your shyness? It's simple. I've been there. Some days, I'm still there. I wanted to write this book to remind myself of the steps I need to take daily to conquer my shyness and obtain self-confidence but I also wanted to share my secrets with all of you. Shyness is not a disease. There is nothing wrong with you. There are varying levels of shyness, and sometimes if it is too overwhelming then you may need to seek the advice of medical professionals. I've found, however, that most forms of shyness can be improved, if not completely controlled, by using the simple tips and tricks I have outlined in this book. If you are willing to do the work, then you will begin to see the magic working in your life.

So you're shy? That's okay. You should learn to accept it, but don't let it hold you back. The key is to find ways to feel self-confident most of the time. You no longer need to let your shyness control your life, or define who you are.

Let's break the chains and determine how you can free your spirit to become an unshackled soul. I want you to bring what's on the inside out, and let your light shine. A wise woman, Kathleen, once told me that when you believe in yourself, you will soar beyond your dreams.

Ready, set, soar!

Chapter 1: Pushing beyond the fear

"You gain strength, courage and confidence by every experience in which you really stop to look fear in the face. 'I lived through this horror. I can take the next thing that comes along.' You must do the thing you think you cannot do."

~ Eleanor Roosevelt.

Fear is a funny thing; it can hold us back, immobilize us, and set us free. When you are shy, pushing beyond the fear is something you will need to learn how to do. Fear is what holds you back from experiencing life's grandest moments, and from achieving your goals and aspirations. Fear is what allows you to remain in your space of shyness.

A little bit of fear is good if you channel it properly. However, fear, when left unchecked can be overwhelming and have devastating impacts on your life. As Henry Ford once said, "One who fears failure limits his activities. Failure is only the opportunity to more intelligently begin again." It is through attempting things and failing that we learn what we need to change to have a greater shot at success the next time.

Let's talk about good fear. Good fear is the kind of nervousness you get before a speaking engagement, or a sporting event. A dear friend, Susan, once told me, a little bit of fear or nervousness is good because it means you are just nervous enough to care if you do well or not. If you are a bit nervous then it means the task at hand is important to you. You can then channel that nervous energy into positive energy, and work as hard as you can to be prepared for the challenge that lies ahead.

If you are so nervous that you become physically sick, then you may need to develop some coping mechanisms and put a plan in place to deal with these feelings and ailments when they arise. The greater the level of your discomfort and nervousness, the more prevalent the physical symptoms may be. In order to deal with this fear you need to be able to tell when it is first coming on. When you get the very first sign of feeling nervous, do something about it. If you don't act immediately then it can quickly spiral out of control and you will give up on the task at hand, and miss out on the opportunity you were hoping to gain.

Act now. Relax. Focus on your breathing. Ask yourself why you are feeling nervous. Begin to reassure yourself. You could meditate, talk to a friend, pray, write out your feelings, try saying positive affirmations, or any technique that will help you reach a calmer state.

You could even seek counselling. There is no shame in this. I used to think counselling was a bad thing, and it wasn't until I sought help that I realized the benefits it could offer. Basically, a counselor offers an outside and objective perspective, and can help you to realize your thought patterns, and give you tools and tactics to make the required changes in your life.

Do any number of things you can think of to make yourself feel better, and then just do it. Just jump into whatever you are doing and let go of those feelings. The fear won't follow you unless you let it. You may still retain a bit of fear, but just ensure it's the healthy kind, the kind that will propel you into an even greater level of success.

Fear is the manifestation of all of those limiting thoughts that are swimming around in your head. Stop listening to them. Push them away. You can do this by recognizing when they are creeping in, and focusing on your breathing. Next, you should take those negative thoughts and rewrite them in a positive form. We have a tendency to believe that our thoughts are out of our control. If we learn that we create our thoughts, and our thoughts shape our experiences, then we will have learned how to take control of our own lives. Those limiting thoughts don't deserve a place inside your head-space anymore.

You must push beyond the fear and do the things you want

to do in your life. You may be thinking that this is easier said than done, and I agree, so the next chapter is devoted to talking more about dealing with and mastering fear.

Chapter 2: Mastering fear

"Courage is resistance to fear, mastery of fear, not absence of fear."

~ Mark Twain

Fear is the biggest obstacle that holds us back from achieving our goals. The type of fear you feel when you are shy or anxious is a different kind of fear. Edmund J. Bourne, Ph.D., discusses fear and anxiety in his book The Anxiety & Phobia Workbook (4th ed.). He differentiates fear in this way, "When you experience anxiety, on the other hand, you often can't specify what it is you're anxious about. The focus of anxiety is more internal than external. It seems to be a response to a vague, distant, or even unrecognized danger. You might be anxious about "losing control" of yourself, or some situation. Or you might feel a vague anxiety about "something bad happening." With that being said, the focus of anxiety is internal, therefore, it only makes sense that the work we need to do to master our fears is internal as well.

There are several changes you can make in your life that will have an impact on your ability to master the fear that you feel. You should work on the physical, emotional, mental and spiritual aspects of yourself. Physical well-being and body image are important when you are dealing with anxiety or shyness. Physical health and a sense of personal well-being are important for your self-esteem.

It's hard to feel good about yourself and able to put your best foot forward when you feel weak or run-down physically. The more you exercise, relax, eat right, and generally take care of your body, the better you will feel about yourself. It will create a ripple effect into the other aspects of your life.

It is also necessary to dress for success. Never under

estimate the power of appearance. You may wish to think that physical appearance is just superficial and that it shouldn't matter, but the truth is that it *is* important. What is important though is not that it matters to others, but how it affects you and your self-esteem. When you feel down and out of touch with yourself it's easy to dress frumpy and without putting much thought into what you are wearing. However, even if you don't feel confident, dress like you are. Dress like you care about yourself, and you will find that your feelings begin to mirror your appearance.

I would often try to dress down or blend in amongst others through the way I presented myself. As I was so shy I just didn't feel the need to be noticed. However, I've come to realize that you can't hide from life. You can't go through life being invisible and not allowing others to see you, because like it or not they will see you. Why not dress your best? You need to really put some thought into how you want to present yourself to the world. Why not let your appearance reflect your inner beauty? Play to your strengths in every thing you do.

You should also nurture your emotional side. It is hard to truly know who you are when you are out of touch with how you feel. It is important to do regular check-ins with yourself to see how you are feeling. It is also important to be able to express the full extent of your emotions. When you can become acquainted with your true desires, dreams, and needs then you will literally begin to feel a weight lifted off of you and you will begin to walk through life with more confidence.

Learning to express your feelings to others takes time. It requires patience on your part, and on the part of others. It takes courage to be vulnerable, even if it's with people you are able to trust. You should choose to surround yourself with people who understand that you are a work in progress and that you might need a little time to work through things before being able to bring them to the surface and share them.

In order to take care of your mental well-being you need to focus on your thoughts. Self-talk is an imperative step in mastering fear. What you tell yourself and your beliefs about yourself most definitely inform your self-esteem. If you feel unworthy and powerless, it is only because you have been telling yourself you are. You need to change the tape that you allow to play in your mind. Change the way you think and create positive self-talk. If you've been telling yourself a story that paints you in a negative light then you need to change that. Change it now. Start by affirming positive thoughts for yourself.

You should start by saying things like:

- I am capable and strong
- I accept myself as I am, and believe I can do anything
- My feelings and needs are important, the more I give to myself the more I can give to others

Your spiritual side is important to nurture as well. Having something to believe in makes us feel connected to someone or something outside of ourselves. It gives us something to reach for, and something to aspire to. Spirituality can help us to feel a sense of purpose and a sense of belonging in this world. It encourages us to delve deeper into our understanding of ourselves, and to bring our own unique identity to the forefront of our lives.

As you know fear never completely diminishes from our lives. There is always that bit of nagging fear that follows us. However, as Bill Cosby said, you need to "decide that you want it more than you are afraid of it." Are you willing to let go of your fear in order to live your best life? You can do it. You can let go just enough to act on your dreams. The rewards you will reap from taking that leap of faith will far outweigh the results of your inaction, and the feeling will become contagious.

Chapter 3: Don't let your shyness define you.

I don't want to get to the end of my life and find that I lived just the length of it. I want to have lived the width of it as well.

~ Diane Ackerman

It is important to realize that it is okay to be shy. There is nothing wrong with you. You aren't abnormal. You certainly aren't the only person to experience it. People have a tendency to say, "Don't be shy." Well...if only it were that simple right? If you knew how to stop being shy then you would! Being shy means that you are afraid of what others think of you, you are afraid of failure, and you feel inferior to others in some way. You are probably eager to succeed in life, but this fear is holding you back. It's great that you want to succeed, and that you care what others think of you, but it's not okay that those thoughts control your behaviour and the way you approach life.

If you're shy to the point where you are avoiding opportunities that could make your life better, then it's time to make some changes. You don't want your introversion to make you dislike yourself, or make you have regrets. How many times have you wanted to join in on an activity or do something, but you decided you were too shy and opted out? This is the problem with shyness. If it immobilizes you and holds you back from achieving your dreams, or exploring your interests, then that is not good for your self-image or your overall quality of life. It is okay to be cautious. Sometimes it can be a quality that saves your life, but if you never take any chances then you will never grow.

For instance, if you want to be a writer, you can't just

dream about publishing a book and think that eventually you will do it. You need to dedicate yourself to your craft. You should write honestly and fearlessly every day. You should write when you have something to say, and write when you feel like you have nothing to say at all. Write as many words as it takes to tell your story. Then, even when you think you are done, you must write some more. You may fear that you will not be good enough, and that nobody will want to read your book, but if you don't take a leap of faith and actually write it, you will never know how you will feel and how others will receive it.

People sometimes have a way of pointing out your shyness, which can make things worse. People used to always comment on the fact that my face had gone from its normal skin tone, to a shade of red. That's not helpful at all, but it happens. Note to extroverts: When dealing with an introvert, try to not let them know that you know they are shy. In doing so, you will be letting that person know that you see beyond their shyness. It will show them that you are genuinely interested in what they have to say, and you are not bothered by the fact that they are nervous about expressing themselves. It will give them a sense of security, and they will be willing to open up to you.

As a shy person, you will need to deal with your insecurities, and work through the awkwardness. The more you think about it and dwell on it, the more you will allow yourself to stay in that space of shyness. Don't let your shyness define you.

Was I painfully shy? Yes. Would those who've met me in recent years agree, particularly when I'm in my "element"? No, probably not. Do I still feel shy sometimes? Absolutely. Do I feel confident in myself? Not always. Can I act like I am? Definitely. Can I "fake it until I make it?" Yes. Confidence is an attitude, and if you don't have it, act like you have it and it will quickly be within your grasp.

When learning to not let your timidity define you, it is important to consider why you won't allow it to any longer. Is it holding you back from doing things you want to try or experience? Is it preventing you from meeting and connecting with new people? Is it stopping you from being who you truly are and becoming who you want to become? If you've answered yes to any or all of these questions, then you may just be ready to change.

You should develop one major goal that will be your focus. For me, the goal was happiness and enjoying life more. If your shyness is holding you back from achieving happiness, then you need to find a way to rid yourself of it. Try something new. Step out of your comfort zone. You will feel uncomfortable at first, but over time it will get easier! Your life will be rich with possibilities, and you won't feel like you are your own biggest obstacle any longer. You need to keep telling yourself that you are deserving of happiness. Once you feel worthy of happiness, then you can more easily take the steps to achieve it.

Please say this with me. Repeat it three times now, and three times daily from now on. "I will no longer let my shyness control me. I am deserving of happiness. I am confident and self-assured."

There you have it. You've taken your first step to becoming a more beautiful, brighter and confident you.

As Diane Ackerman asserts, she doesn't want to get to the end of her life and realize she's only lived the length of it and not the width of it. We should all endeavor to live expansive lives. The time to begin making the small changes necessary to live your life out loud is now. Don't wait until you get to the end of your life and look back with regret. Live now. Choose moment by moment who you want to be and share that self with the world.

Chapter 4: Developing Self-Awareness

"Our deepest wishes are whispers of our authentic selves. We must learn to respect them. We must learn to listen."

~ Sarah Ban Breathnach

The first step to shedding your shyness is developing self-awareness. If you know what makes you feel shy, or self-conscious in certain situations, then you can begin to figure out ways to shift your behaviour. If you know who you are then you can be yourself with much more confidence.

You should begin by taking personal inventories. Be inquisitive. Who are you? What do you excel at? What makes you unique?

Delve as deeply as you can into the essence of your being. If you can begin to develop a relationship with yourself, then you will quickly learn what you need to be happy. You will know what makes you happy because you will be in touch with your feelings. You will know why you feel certain emotions and how your experiences shape your life if you do some self-exploration. You will also be in a better position to demand respect. When you feel confident with yourself, then you will only accept a certain level of treatment from others. That level gets proportionately higher as your level of self-confidence rises.

If you can spend some time thinking about your feelings then you will have a greater sense of what fears are causing your shyness. Are you afraid of what others might think of you? Are you afraid of failing? Are you blaming your circumstances or those around you?

When you are shy you have a tendency to over-think situations, and often your mind wanders and lands on the worst case scenario. If I do that, then he might not like me. If I do this, then I am going to feel embarrassed. It is important to ask yourself, what is the worst that could happen? If I ask someone if they are hiring, they might say no. Yes, they might, but at least you took the initiative to ask. The next time they are hiring, they will think of you, and remember that you took a chance and expressed your interest.

It is important to think about the downside of things only to convince yourself that it's really not that bad, but do yourself a favour, don't dwell on it. Once you establish the answer to what's the worst that could happen, then you need to let it go. Free your mind of that worry because will it really matter ten minutes, ten hours, ten years down the road? Probably not. The more risks you take, the more you will begin to feel comfortable in your ability to do so. As the saying goes, practice makes perfect. It most certainly makes things easier.

Remember that at every point along your journey you need to reward yourself. You've made it this far in life, and you will go much further. Congratulate yourself on the little successes because each one is contributing to your overall journey towards self-confidence.

Now that you know who you are, take care of yourself. Learn how to nourish yourself. Take time to do the things that make you happy. Surround yourself with people who build you up. It is important to have a network of supportive people in your life.

Figure out what types of activities lift you up, help you relax, and help you to become more in tune with yourself. Perhaps you could take a relaxing bath. Maybe you could benefit from half an hour of meditation. You could pick a great book to read. You can do anything that makes you feel fulfilled.

"Me time" is important. "Me time" means taking a time out from life. Quietly remove yourself from the distractions of your life. Find a quiet space in your home or in your workplace to just sit quietly for a few moments. It is important to do this because it is through silence that we can journey inward for strength and knowledge about ourselves. It's hard to navigate who you are when you are so wrapped up in the demands of your life. If you can create time each day to commit to your job, your spouse, your children, then you can most certainly create time for you.

As you become older you quickly learn that "me time" becomes nearly impossible to obtain. You have work commitments, family commitments, and so many other things in your way. However, you can always steal a few moments for yourself each day, and that is all it takes. I like to take my moments to myself in the car as I'm driving to work. I can reflect on my way to work about how I want my day to unfold. I can practice positive self-talk and affirmations (more about these in a later chapter). I can listen to motivational music or recordings. I can pump myself up; get excited about my day, and my life. Another way I squeeze in my "me time" is by waking up earlier than the rest of my family members. I use the quiet morning hours to do my writing, reflect on my life, and work on my dream journal or anything else I might feel like doing for myself.

In the above quotation from Sarah Ban Breathnach she talks about our soul's whisper. We all have an inner voice and if we silence ourselves long enough we will hear it. This is what you will hear if you begin the practice of "me time". By silencing our thoughts, the noise and clutter in our minds, we can listen for that guiding voice inside of us. Take direction from that voice. It's your beautiful soul asking you to honour its wishes.

Chapter 5: Join In

"Nobody cares if you can't dance well. Just get up and dance. Great dancers are not great because of their technique; they are great because of their PASSION."
~ Martha Graham

When you are shy it can be extremely difficult to find the courage to join in on activities. You will be afraid of what others might think of you, how you will look, and you may think you are not good enough. We have a tendency as humans to always think we are not good enough, or that we are less than others. This is not the case. The only things holding us back are our thoughts. Our thoughts create the fear that prevents us from taking action in our lives.

Are you scared to try out for the basketball team? Do it anyway. What do you have to lose? If you try out and don't make it, then you are no further behind than if you hadn't tried, and you will have taken a positive step in your development. You put yourself out there, and you did your best to make things happen for yourself. If you don't try then you don't even have a chance to see if you could have made it. You will be depriving yourself of the opportunity to do what you want to do. Whether you make the team or not, congratulate yourself. Give yourself credit for doing something that was outside of your comfort zone. You will feel good about your decision to try and will be more likely to try something new again in the future.

Let me give you a personal example. I was a basketball lover when I was younger. I would play for hours each night in my driveway, to work on my skills, practice my shots, and I would always coerce my sisters who were less enthused about basketball to join me. If I had at least one other player to play with then I could also work on my defensive skills. I played basketball every year in elementary school. In grade 8, I even signed up for a league outside of school called "Little NBA". I was terrified to try out, but my elementary school coach insisted I try and said it would be good for me to further develop my skills if I wanted to play in high school. I decided to go for it, even though I was terrified.

During try-outs there were very few girls there. This instantly made me feel nervous. Despite my anxiety, I went through all of the try-outs, and I kept watching the other players. They seemed bigger, stronger and more talented than me. I started to feel as if I didn't belong there. I thought I had made a mistake in even trying out. In spite of these feelings of inadequacy, the developing lump in my throat and the sinking feeling in my heart, I continued on.

Then, something incredible happened. I made the team! It happened to be that I was the only girl on my team. It was scary. I thought, there is no way I'm ever going to be as good as the boys. They aren't going to pass me the ball, and I'll never get a chance to prove I can play. Well for the first few games, that is what happened. I didn't get many passes, and I didn't get many opportunities to shoot. However, I kept calling for the ball and making myself open to receiving passes.

One night a parent yelled from the stands, "Pass it to the girl!" One boy listened. He passed it to me. I took a shot and scored. What a triumphant moment. From that moment on, the boys realized that I could play well. They passed me the ball more. I finally felt a sense of belonging. I now knew I deserved to be there.

See what can happen when you put yourself out there? I was terrified. I remained nervous before and during every single game, but, I did it! I learned what it feels like to join in. I was becoming an active participant in making my dreams come true.

I continued to join activities and groups throughout my time in high school and university. It took a lot of courage each and every time. It did get easier the more I did it. There are still opportunities I wish I had taken, but for the most part those regrets are minor ones. However, had I tapped into these secrets sooner, then I'm confident I wouldn't have any regrets

18

or missed opportunities at all.

Let me give you one example. From grade nine, I always admired students who joined Student Council. I thought it looked like a lot of fun, but I kept listening to the running dialogue in my head that said... You can't do that. You are too shy. You'd be embarrassed too easily. The rest of the students will eat you alive if you even attempt it. That voice is not you. Don't listen to it. That voice is made up of egotistical nonsense, and societal influences that you no longer need to bother even listening to. You need to develop a new voice (more on how to do that in a later chapter).

Finally, in grade twelve, my final year of high school, I mustered up the courage to join the Student Council. It was the most amazing experience of my high school years. I met lots of new friends, and learned some important new skills. I wished I had joined in grade nine so that I could have experienced it sooner. This is why it is so important to take action in your life. You need to participate relentlessly in your own happiness. You will be able to discover more about yourself by trying new activities. It may lead you to discover what you are passionate about, and perhaps what you want to do with your life.

Chapter 6: Acting & Affirmations

"You are as amazing as you let yourself be. Let me repeat that. You are as amazing as you let yourself be."
~Elizabeth Alraune

One very important step in gaining self-confidence, is acting the part. Even if you don't feel confident, act as if you are. It will help teach you what being confident feels like, and will provide a coping mechanism for those times when your self-confidence is fleeting. You've probably heard the saying, "fake it until you make it." This applies to confidence as well. If you can act like you have it regularly, then eventually it will become so deep-rooted that it will stick and you'll be able to manifest that trait in your real life. Practice the words, actions and thoughts of a confident person.

Here are some affirmations to get you started.

I am a confident and loving person, and I attract others who are the same.

I believe in myself, and I am living according to my dreams.

I am brave, I am strong, and I am secure in my beliefs.

I am in tune with my deepest inner thoughts. I chose to listen to the ones that will guide me to where I want to be.

I will no longer care what others think of me. It is what I think of me that matters.

I am enough. I am destined to do great things.

These are just a few that I came up with off the top of my head. There are many affirmations available online and from various other self-help books if you are lost on where to begin, or do not feel comfortable creating your own just yet. Louise L. Hay is the queen of affirmations, and so I suggest turning to her books as a starting point. Here are a few of her creations that I just love:

All is well in my world.

When I find harmony and balance in my mind, I find it in my life.

I allow each day to show me the beauty of a new life. I am at peace.

I am a divine, magnificent expression of Life. Everything I need to know comes to me. I am protected and guided...

I comfortably and easily release the old and welcome the new in my life. I am safe.

For more of her affirmations you could follow her on Twitter, or check out any number of her books. They can be found on her website, www.louisehay.com. I personally recommend her book, "You Can Heal Your Life".

Affirmations are hugely important in making the necessary changes to our self-image. They are one of the methods through which we can learn to love ourselves. You will undoubtedly feel stupid for saying these things, or feel like you shouldn't be talking to yourself. You may even feel like you are being self-righteous. Let go of those beliefs. Just drop them from your mind. Self-confidence and self-love are not self-righteous exercises. They are ways of nurturing our souls, and taking care of our emotional, physical, spiritual and mental well-being. Nothing is more important than your health, and so you should treat it as a top priority in your life.

If you don't feel comfortable saying affirmations in front of anyone, then do it at a time when you can be alone. Do it as you are getting ready in front of the mirror in the morning, or at night before you go to sleep. Do it in your car while you drive. You can write them down, but it is also necessary to say them to yourself aloud so that they firmly plant themselves in your subconscious.

Keeping a journal is another great activity to help ensure you are keeping your spiritual well-being in check. You could keep a journal of affirmations, or any other items important for your personal development. I keep a gratitude journal and a dream journal for myself. I also keep a marriage journal with my husband. It can become easy to be trapped in negativity mode. If you start keeping track of what you are thankful for, what you aspire to do, and your relationship with others you will be able to dwell in positivity and possibilities.

Another thing you should do is smile! A smile is a very important part of acting the part of a confident person and exuding a confident attitude. A smile can do a number of things for self-confidence. It can enhance your outward appearance, and make you look more approachable. As shy people we often come across as stand-offish or unapproachable, not because we are, but just because of how our behaviours are perceived by others.

If you are a shy person then you may be ultra-aware of this misconception, and it may further contribute to feelings of self-consciousness. A way to get around it is to smile. A smile can lift your mood, and will lift the mood of those around you. It will put you at ease, and allow you the chance to act and speak with confidence. Others may see you smile, and automatically be drawn to you. It could encourage them to start a conversation with you, which makes it easier for you if you don't have the courage to start a conversation with them. Once you've begun to flash your smile, you should learn to focus on your breathing. Breathing is a very good way to control your central nervous system.

Let's talk about another important technique you can use to control how you feel in social situations. If you feel yourself getting anxious, focus on your breathing. When we become nervous our breath becomes shorter. In order to change this, we must be acutely aware of our breathing patterns. In order to do this, we must consciously take time to assess them and become aware of them by bringing out attention to our breath. Pause, take a moment, gather your thoughts, and take a deep breath, then another, then another, then another, until you feel ready to proceed. Another technique I have learned is to breathe in while saying (in your head) R...E...and breathe out while intoning L...A...X, to spell the word relax. This action allows you to remind yourself to relax, but also by drawing out the word you are ensuring your breath is deeper.

If you use the above techniques you will automatically start to approach things from a deeper level. You will come from a calmer state of awareness, and you can drown out the voices that say you can't do something.

Chapter 7: Perfection is a Mirage

"The thing that is really hard, and really amazing, is giving up on being perfect and beginning the work of becoming yourself."

~ Anna Quindlen

Perfection is a mirage. Really, it doesn't exist. We chase it, and think that it's something we can attain. We can't. If you must attach a definition to perfection, or want something to strive for then here's my definition; Perfection means being the absolute best you that you can be. This definition gives you something to strive for an ongoing commitment to self-improvement. The only one you can and ever should be competing with is you.

Perfection is like fear. It can immobilize us, and make us feel inferior. You may begin to think, well if I can't do it perfectly, why even bother trying. If I can't talk to someone in public without feeling shy, then why try? Again, you need to stop those limiting thoughts from bubbling up from your subconscious. You need to replace them with new thoughts. These new thoughts are positive ones. You need to start thinking thoughts like these: I am a work in progress. I try my best every day in every way. I can do anything I set out to do.

Everyone experiences setbacks. You must learn to embrace the awkward. Even the most seemingly confident individuals experience awkwardness. They might trip and fall in a public place, or have an awkward conversation with a peer. It happens, don't worry about it. Alexander Pope, the English poet, once said, "To err is human; to forgive, divine." Forgive yourself. Allow yourself to make mistakes, learn from them and move on. There will be many times when life knocks you down; the true test of the strength of your character is how you react to it. Will you allow it to keep you down, or will you jump up fighting?

You owe it to yourself to try new things, meet new people, and be the best you that you can be. Don't let the fear of being less than perfect stand in your way. Perfection, like fear, is a manifestation of those limiting thoughts that you are thinking. Let it go. Move on. Embrace the awkward. Look for the lesson. What can a certain experience teach you? How can you change your behaviors next time so that the experience is more enjoyable for you? How can you shift your attitude to allow for some room to grow?

The first definition of success that comes to my mind is setting out a goal for myself, a time frame in which I will achieve it, and then taking the action required to complete the task. I am sure many others think this way as well. Sometimes though, I believe that success is measured by the chances we take. Even if we have taken chances and don't "succeed" according to normal (another mirage) standards, is it still success? I believe it is. It can still be seen as a small triumph and we should congratulate ourselves for having the courage to try. If we hadn't tried we would definitely not be further ahead.

Trying and not succeeding is an important part of our development too. It teaches us patience, perseverance, and forgiveness. We must forgive ourselves for falling short; have patience that we will get another chance at it, and persevere to create more opportunities for ourselves. A friend of mine, Kim, told me that her definition of success is, "If it gave you joy, then you were successful." I love this definition. It's a great way to think about success.

Always remember that perfection is a mirage, and if you continually chase it or allow it to immobilize you, then you are only cheating yourself out of opportunities to let your light shine.

Chapter 8: Believe in Yourself

"Our deepest fear is not that we are inadequate. Our deepest fear is that we are powerful beyond measure. It is our light, not our darkness, that most frightens us. We ask ourselves, who am I to be brilliant, gorgeous, talented, fabulous? Actually, who are you not to be?"
~Marianne Williamson

Self-belief is one of the single most important factors in developing self-confidence. If you believe in yourself then anything is possible. You will have unlimited potential, and will have the courage to take chances in life. Self-belief can take a lot of time to develop, and like anything we've talked about to this point, it takes practice. The great philosopher and thinker Aristotle once said, "Knowing yourself is the beginning of all wisdom". Self-knowledge, and then, self-belief is the key that can unlock all of the doors to greatness in your life.

Self-belief means being your own cheerleader. You need to know how to pump yourself up, keep yourself motivated, and know without a doubt that you can achieve what you set your mind to. You might be saying, well that sounds great, but where do I even begin? Here are some tips.

Focus on your thoughts. For, as Buddha said, "The mind is everything. What you think you become." As we've talked about in previous chapters, our thoughts are the mind-map of our lives. They predict how we will approach tasks, and how we will react to them. If we want to change our lives, then we must first change our thinking. If you are constantly focusing on the negative, then negative is what you will get. If you focus on the positive, then positive is what you get. Some people call this the law of attraction. I like to call it the law of intention. You aren't attracting anything; you are intentionally seeking it out by changing the course of your thoughts. If you change your thoughts then your actions will follow. If you are constantly thinking about how you will achieve things then your thoughts will propel your body to action.

There are many ways in which you can begin to change your thoughts. The starting point is to track them. In order to know what you must change, you need to know what your current patterns are. Start a thought journal. When you are feelings overwhelmed by a certain situation, step back, and take a few moments to pause and figure out what thoughts are running through your mind. Write them down. If they are negative, simply strike them out with your pen, and re-write them in a positive form. Then read those thoughts aloud and repeat as many times as you deem necessary. If you repeat them enough, they will stick. You can repeat this exercise as often as you like. It is a minor investment of time, which will offer many benefits.

Another important aspect to developing self-belief is energy. You need to be aware of the energy that people give to you. Only surround yourself with those people who bring gifts of positive energy. You cannot control the type of energy that people bring to you, but you can control what you do with it. You can either accept it, or graciously decline. Over time other peoples' energy can really weigh on us, if we allow it to. Don't allow it to.

For example, if you are in a relationship and you are constantly feeling that the other person's energy is bringing you down then you need to do something about it. Maybe you need to move on, but maybe you can just command the type of treatment you require. Sometimes all it takes is you signalling to that person what you are willing to accept. If they choose to continue on the path they are on that is their choice, and your choice is whether or not you can continue on your path with them by your side.

If the person that is bringing you negative energy is someone that you are unable to separate yourself from, say a parent or other relative, then you need to resolve to maintain control over your own energy. Continue on in a positive manner regardless of how they try to make you feel. In the constant navigation of yourself, you may find that the people you choose to surround yourself may change. You may require different types of people in your life at different points in time, and that is okay. True self-belief means that you are able to uphold your own standards and sense of self regardless of what others do. Be your most beautiful self, for as Marrianne Williamson says, "who are you not to be?"

Chapter 9: Change Your Attitude, Change Your Life

"What I like most about change is that it's a synonym for 'hope.' If you are taking a risk, what you are really saying is, 'I believe in tomorrow, and I will be part of it.'" ~ *Linda Ellerbee*

Often in life we like to think that things happen to us, and that we are at the mercy of our circumstances. I know I'm guilty of that type of thinking as well. Things do not happen to us, we make them happen. The thought process we use to make things happen is what determines the type of experiences that come our way. If you change your attitude, and way of thinking, to be more positive, you will attract more positive things into your life. Remember my law of intention I talked about in the previous chapter? If you intentionally shift your attitude then you will attract great things.

How should you begin to change your attitude? You can use many of the tools we've talked about so far. You can monitor and record your thoughts, replacing them with positive ones. You can practice positive affirmations. You can do some self-exploration to determine what causes your attitudes and thought processes. You should find out what or who influences you. Is it a positive or negative energy being delivered to you? Will you accept it or not? Remember you are in control of the energy you choose to accept. If someone around you is negative it can be extremely hard not to follow suit, but the choice is always yours. If their negativity becomes too much to take, then you may need to walk away.

If you can't walk away because the negativity is coming from a source that is too close to you, then you need to remember that their thoughts don't need to become your thoughts. Raise the volume of your own voice so much that is drowns out theirs. You can listen to someone else respectfully without agreeing with them. You just need to resolve to be positive even in the face of negativity because you are sure to encounter it throughout your life.

You need to surround yourself with people who will build you up. It is the hardest thing in the world to share your dreams with others. You can be selective about who you share them with. Always be prepared for naysayers. There will always be those that say you cannot do something. It's up to you to decide whether or not you will listen to them. Choose to drown out their thoughts with your positive ones. Drawn upon your own self-belief for strength. You are the only one who can set limits for yourself, and so why not explore limitless possibilities within your life. You deserve it.

Another important thing you can do to change your attitude is to act like a positive person or model yourself after a positive person. Acting and modeling aren't just for celebrities. You can be a celebrity of your own life by acting and modeling the behavior and attitudes you want to exude. You can often pick up on various techniques from watching others and emulating them. Of course, always keep yourself at the heart of all of it. Remember that you are uniquely you, and that you may need to adapt their techniques slightly to suit yourself.

In the next chapters we will discuss some more concrete ways through which you can change your attitude and shift your thinking. We will learn about the importance of a dream journal, and a gratitude journal. By being thankful for what we have and having a clear sight of our dreams we can work towards achieving the life we are meant to live. Changing our thoughts can feel risky and scary because it is unfamiliar territory. As Linda Ellerbee says, to take a risk is to say, "I believe in tomorrow, and I will be part of it."

Chapter 10: Building a Dream Journal

"The reason it matters to care passionately about something is that it whittles the world down to a more manageable size. It makes the world seem not huge and empty but full of possibility."

~ Susan Orlean

Dreams and aspirations are an extremely important aspect of our personal development as humans. If you don't have any, get some! Start thinking about all of the things you'd like to achieve in your life. Then you need to create a visual representation of them. Make a collage with pictures or words to illustrate or describe the things you want in your life. It can be material things such as a sports car, or a new bike. It can be a sum of money you'd like to earn. It can be a career aspiration or anything else of your choosing.

Once you create this visual representation then you need to hang it somewhere where you will see it every day. Hang it in your home, your office, your locker at school, your bedroom. Put it anywhere where you can look at it often. The purpose of this dream collage is to implant in your subconscious all of your dreams. The theory is that what you think about will become yours. Some people believe that this is the only step you need to take, and because you are seeing these images every day your subconscious will automatically search for ways to make them attainable.

I say, why not give your subconscious a boost, and write a dream journal to accompany your dream collage. A dream journal does a couple of different things. First, it allows you to express in writing what it is you hope to achieve or obtain. Secondly, it allows you to write out an exact plan of action of how you will go about achieving these things. You can list your goals, and the steps you will need to take to obtain them.

I will provide some examples. My dream journal consists of publishing a book (and several more books), buying myself a truck, taking a workshop with Habitat for Humanity and then building a house with them. I have many other goals and aspirations that I haven't listed here as well. Here are some concrete steps I can take to achieve my goals.

To publish a book, I will need to think of an idea. Write every day. Search for publishing companies. Find out where I want to market it, and how I will do that. I will want to plan out speaking engagements to get my book out there. Sometimes if the goal is an immediate one then you should give yourself a time frame for completion to keep yourself on track. If I want to publish a book by December 25, 2012, then I will need to be a lot stricter on the deadline I set for myself. By the way, if this book you are reading now is published before this date, then I will have succeeded in attaining one of my major goals in my dream journal.

The goal of buying myself a truck is more of a distant goal for me. I don't need a truck right now, and it's not practical because I've just begun this early stage of parenthood, and a car or van suits my needs better. I have an excellent car right now. I want a truck as a luxury for when I am older. So I am setting a goal of buying myself a truck when I turn fifty. I don't really need to write out specific steps yet on how I will do it. I could however, go to a dealership, try out the trucks that I like, get a brochure of the one I want, and include it in my dream collage.

The goal of building a house with Habitat for Humanity also requires work. I can't just expect that it will happen. I need to take action. First, I would need to register for a workshop with them to learn construction skills. I may want to talk to others who've participated in the program to learn about their experiences. I could attend an information seminar at the Habitat for Humanity centre. Then I need to just do it. I will become a volunteer.

These are some of my personal examples of my dream collage/dream journal. I really do feel the two exercises go hand-in-hand and that both are necessary for your successful achievement of your dreams.

Start your dream journal today; make sure to include the dream collage, and the written part. You can collect images from magazines, the Internet, brochures, and more. Make sure you dedicate some time each day to reviewing your dreams. Even if you only have time to look at the collage it will provide a trigger to remind you of the goals that you wrote down. You should review your dream journal weekly or monthly to ensure that you are taking positive steps towards your dreams.

Remember, half the battle of achieving the life you want is envisioning your dreams, and the other half is acting on them. In this dream journal exercise you have the opportunity to do both. My dream journal has assisted me in achieving many goals so far in my life. Some of which included getting married, starting a family, completing both my undergraduate and graduate degrees, and becoming a writer. All of these thing which were once images and thoughts in my dream journal are now my realities.

Discover what it is you feel passionately about and set out ways in which you can begin living that passion. Follow your bliss.

Chapter 11: Two powerful Words. Thank you.

"The single greatest thing you can do to change your life today would be to start being grateful for what you already have right now. And the more grateful you are, the more you get." ~ Oprah Winfrey

This chapter is dedicated to the importance of gratitude in our lives. I didn't realize the full magnitude of the concept that Oprah describes in the quotation above, until it happened in my life.

I had a good paying, highly sought after job, and in everyone's eyes I should have been lucky to have it. I was lucky, and I considered it a blessing, but at the time, specifically in the last year I was there, I was miserable. I hated getting up and going to work each day. I blamed my circumstances. If only I had more money, I wouldn't need to rely on this job to pay my bills. If only I had chosen a different path, then I wouldn't be here still.

My mom, who is a firm believer in gratitude, and keeps a daily gratitude journal, encouraged me to do the same. She went out and bought me a journal. I used a gratitude journal during this time, but also through some very dark times in my past, and it carried me through. I had just forgotten the importance of it, and I am so very grateful that she reminded me.

As soon as I was able to be thankful and accept what I had, it made room for greater things to happen in my life. I learned to appreciate my job, not because I loved it or even liked it but because of what it had done for me. It gave me a chance to learn, to become more confident, to gain important communication and people skills, meet some amazing people, it paid my bills, it even provided a top-up pay when I was on maternity leave with my son. Without this, I wouldn't have been able to enjoy a full year at home with him while he was a baby. My financial circumstances would have dictated that I return to work sooner. It also provided me with an income while I completed my Master's program part-time through distance education. So once I started to think of all of these benefits, going to work each day became easier, and I was a much happier person for it. I still wanted to get out of that job, but this time, instead of finding excuses, I found solutions!

The next steps that happened in my life are truly amazing. My husband was struggling to find work, and more specifically, work that he enjoyed. He applied for opportunities everywhere. Then one day, he received a call about a job in a different city. We took an almost 4 hour trip for the interview, it seemed to go well, and then very shortly after, he was offered the job. The decision was fairly easy for us, because the job was well-paying, and was what he wanted to do. The only thing was we would need to relocate. I couldn't leave my job because we relied on my income to support us. So he took the job and only came home on weekends for two and a half months.

I stayed at my job, and asked for a transfer. I was told that at this time there were no immediate transfers available. I eventually decided that we needed to be together as a family, and so I took a giant leap of faith and took a leave from my job to be with my husband, and our son, as a family. We moved to our new town. I didn't have work. I applied for jobs, went to playgroups with my son, started writing this book, and writing for various blogs and companies. I even dabbled in a bit of teaching. I did everything that my soul was calling for me to do. It was the best time of my life. I was happier than I had ever been, but also poorer than I had ever been (financially). It was a tough time, and we are still recovering from it, but it was a rich time for my personal development.

When I was quietly going about doing the things I loved, I got a call from one of the jobs I had applied for. They wanted me to come in for an interview. I said sure, and then a few weeks later, away I went. My interview went extremely well, and the job was in the very field I had been studying in for my Master's degree, so it seemed like a great fit for me. Instead of thinking about my lack of practical experience, and many other reasons why I might not get the job, I remained positive. I kept my focus on gratitude. I was grateful for the opportunity of the interview. I knew my interview went well. I knew I showed them everything about myself that I possibly could in that hour, and I knew they were impressed. I left a great impression. I did my best, and that's all I could ask of myself. I prayed about it, and kept positive all the while. Then, I received a call a short while later asking me to come in and meet the team. I did this, and once again, it was a great experience. I thought maybe they would offer me the job on the spot, but they didn't. One of the managers was away on vacation and so I would need to wait two weeks to hear of their decision. I thought the wait might kill me.

However, after my meeting with the team on a Monday, I got a call on Wednesday. It was the manager that was on holidays. She was trying to be on vacation but kept working instead she admitted. She offered me the job. I originally thought it was a contract job. Then she explained it was permanent, had many benefits, and perks, and she was going to start me at a very high starting pay. The salary was beyond what I ever expected I could make at my age. I couldn't believe it. I still can't believe it. I called my family and friends, all of whom were so happy for me. To them, it was a true testament of faith, hard-work and positive thinking. I had done all of these things, and now finally the job of my dreams was mine. This has all happened within the last few weeks, as I am writing this. I am so pleased to be able to share this story with you right now. It's amazing what life can bring when you believe in yourself. It's amazing that a shy gal like me could attain such great things, so early in life.

Those two powerful words – thank you; have brought me so much more than I ever thought possible. I will never stop being grateful for the things I have in my life, and I want you to do the same. It is through gratitude that we can learn to see the world anew. We can take the time to appreciate the small triumphs and successes in our lives, and that, my friends, is how you achieve greatness.

Let me back track a bit to explain a little bit more about what a gratitude journal is. Basically, all you need to get started is a small journal, a pen, and some thoughts. Each day you should take out your journal and write down three things you are grateful for. There will always be something you are grateful for. Here are some examples. I am grateful for my best friend. I am grateful for a roof over my head. I am grateful for a loving family. These are just a few of the things you could be grateful for.

During times of great struggle in your life when you think you don't have anything to be grateful for there is always something. Some days I would simply write - I am grateful for the sun. Of course, if you can think of more than three things to be grateful for then by all means add them. The more you dwell in gratitude, the more space you create in your life for positive things to come your way.

Conclusion

"Being forced to seek balance within ourselves, we can make our unsteady, stumbling days feel less and less like disaster and more and more like a joyful dance – the dance of a wildly, wonderfully, perfectly unbalanced life." ~ Martha Beck

As we come to a close on our journey of self-discovery together, I'd like to take this time to congratulate you for having the courage to read this book, and take a leap of faith with me. If you commit to the advice and practical solutions I have provided in this book, then you are well on your way to shedding your shyness and achieving the life you've always wanted for yourself.

This book is about taking the beauty you have on the inside, and finding a way for you to express it, and let it shine. This book is about freeing yourself. It's about becoming an unshackled soul who can confidently go forth in the world; conquer your fears, face your truth, and follow your bliss. It's about letting go of the fear that has been holding you back from being all that you can be.

The first step in self-confidence is always self-belief. If you believe that you can achieve anything, then it will be yours. It is my hope that this book will guide you on your quest for self-belief, and will help to propel you to a level of success that is far greater than what you are able to envision for yourself. It's time to embrace the awkward, the almost, the getting there, and respect that you are journeying each day towards a more beautiful and better you.

About The Author

I'd love to hear from you. Please connect with me in any of the following ways to let me know how you are doing on your journey, or if you have any comments or questions for me. Also, if you enjoyed this book please consider leaving a review on Amazon. Thank you so much for your support.

Twitter: @skywaywriter or www.twitter.com/skywaywriter

Websites:
www.lindsaybrantbrumwell.ca, www.brandnewcontent.ca

E-mail: lindsay@lindsaybrantbrumwell.ca, or for freelance writing enquiries lindsay@brandnewcontent.ca

Facebook: Lindsay Brant-Brumwell– Author,
www.facebook.com/lindsaybrantbrumwellauthor***

www.ingramcontent.com/pod-product-compliance
Lightning Source LLC
Chambersburg PA
CBHW060634030426
42337CB00018B/3366